THE
TRUTH
ABOUT
SUCCESS

ABRAMS NOTERIE, NEW YORK

CONTENTS

HOW
DOES ONE
SUCCESSFULLY
INTRODUCE
A BOOK ABOUT
SUCCESS?

I will admit I felt a bit intimidated by this task. As someone who has spent my career researching, writing, and speaking about various elements of career and workplace success, my mind immediately started spinning with the various anecdotes and advice I'd come across over the years.

I wondered, should I write about how different generations often develop different definitions of success? Or expound on the fact that even objectively successful people aren't necessarily successful in every element of their lives? Or perhaps address the differences and similarities between personal success and professional success? Or go back to the basics by looking up the precise definition of "success"? (It is "the accomplishment of an aim or purpose," from the Latin *successus*, if you were wondering.)

Then, finally, I took a deep breath, got out of my own head (and the dictionary), and started reading through all of the wisdom you are about to enjoy. As I absorbed page after page, I found myself amazed by the breadth and depth of the people, ideas, concepts, and actions invoked. Could success—a concept so many of us focus so much energy on—truly encompass all of this diversity and difference? The answer, of course, is an unconditional yes.

From Confucius to Harriet Tubman to Dr. Seuss to Oprah Winfrey and beyond, thinkers and doers of every era have developed and practiced their own definitions of success. Their words are celebratory, inspirational, contradictory, serious, funny, and everything in between. And their guidance will address myriad elements of your life, both personal and professional.

Perhaps what stands out to me most after reading *The Truth About Success* is the vital importance of balance to leading a successful life. You will find axioms about hard work and persistence, but also about laughter and kindness. You will enjoy insights about achievement and growth, but also about dreams and hope. And you may be surprised to find an entire section on the tremendous importance of failure to achieving success.

So, I think the best way to introduce this book is to celebrate the fact that there is no one, single truth about success.

INSTEAD, LIKE A DIAMOND, THIS SMALL BUT VALUABLE WORD CONTAINS A MULTITUDE OF BRILLIANT ANGLES THAT ADD UP TO A STRONG AND BEAUTIFUL WHOLE.

—**Lindsey Pollak**, *New York Times* bestselling author of *Becoming the Boss: New Rules for the Next Generation of Leaders*

The best possible outcome.
Winning the game. Crossing the finish line.
Success can mean many different things, but it means
something to each of us. We determine
what our own success is.

STEVE
JOBS

We're here to make a dent in
the universe. Otherwise why
even be here?

CARL
SANDBURG

I'm an idealist. I don't know where
I'm going, but I'm on my way.

MARGARET
MEAD

Never doubt that a small group of
thoughtful, committed citizens can
change the world. Indeed it is the
only thing that ever has.

SUCCESS IS . . .

HENRY WADSWORTH LONGFELLOW

Not in the clamor of the crowded street,

Not in the shouts and plaudits of the throng,

But in ourselves, are triumph and defeat.

UNKNOWN

DEAR LORD, ALLOW ME TO BE THE MAN MY DOG THINKS I AM.

MARIANNE
WILLIAMSON

Success means we go to sleep at night
knowing that our talents and abilities
were used in a way that served others.

ALBERT
EINSTEIN

Try not to become a man of success
but rather try to become a man of value.
He is considered successful in our day
who gets more out of life than he puts
in. But a man of value will give more
than he receives.

MURIEL STRODE

I will not follow where the path may lead, but I will go where there is no path, and I will leave a trail.

ALBERT SZENT-GYÖRGYI

Research is to see what everybody has seen and think what nobody has thought.

HENRY DAVID THOREAU

It's not what you look at that matters, it's what you see.

SUCCESS IS . . .

MICHAEL KORDA

In order to succeed, we must first believe that we can.

JIM ROHN

If you are not willing to risk the usual, you will have to settle for the ordinary.

GRANTLAND RICE

For when the One Great Scorer comes to write against your name— He marks—not that you won or lost—but how you played the game.

EXPERIENCE LIFE
IN ALL POSSIBLE
WAYS—GOOD/BAD,
BITTER/SWEET,
DARK/LIGHT,
SUMMER/WINTER.
EXPERIENCE ALL
THE DUALITIES.

SUCCESS IS . . .

HARRIET BEECHER STOWE

The bitterest tears shed over graves are for words left unsaid and deeds left undone.

H. JACKSON BROWN JR.

Judge your success by what you had to give up in order to get it.

ROBERT
FROST

Two roads diverged in a wood,
and I—
I took the one less traveled by,
And that has made all the difference.

CARLOS
CASTANEDA

Does this path have a heart?
If it does, the path is good; if it doesn't,
it is of no use.

SUCCESS IS . . .

"Would you tell me, please, which way I ought to go from here?"

"That depends a good deal on where you want to get to," said the [Cheshire] Cat.

"I don't much care where—" said Alice.

"Then it doesn't matter which way you go," said the Cat.

WHAT SEEM TO US BITTER TRIALS ARE OFTEN BLESSINGS IN DISGUISE.

FLORENCE
NIGHTINGALE

I attribute my success to this:—
I never gave or took an excuse.

WILLIAM
SHAKESPEARE

Nothing can come of nothing.

MITCH ALBOM

All endings are also beginnings.
We just don't know it at the time.

DON'T
...

. . . let what you cannot do interfere with what you can do.

BENJAMIN JOHN WOODEN

. . . look back. Something may be gaining on you.

SATCHEL PAIGE

. . . let the fear of losing be greater than the excitement of winning.

ROBERT KIYOSAKI

. . . be distracted by criticism. Remember, the only taste of success some people have is when they take a bite out of you.

ZIG ZIGLAR

RALPH WALDO
EMERSON

Nothing astonishes men so much
as common sense and plain dealing.

WARREN
BUFFETT

Someone's sitting in the shade
today because someone planted
a tree a long time ago.

UNKNOWN

SUCCESS ISN'T JUST ABOUT WHAT YOU ACCOMPLISH IN YOUR LIFE; IT'S ABOUT WHAT YOU INSPIRE OTHERS TO DO.

RALPH WALDO
EMERSON

This time, like all times, is a very good one, if we but know what to do with it.

JOHN C.
MAXWELL

Change is inevitable.
Growth is optional.

ALDOUS
HUXLEY

Experience is not what happens to a man; it is what a man does with what happens to him.

SUCCESS IS . . .

HENRY
CLOUD

We change our behavior when
the pain of staying the same becomes
greater than the pain of changing.

HENRY DAVID
THOREAU

Things do not change; we change.

TOM ROBBINS	To achieve the impossible, it is precisely the unthinkable that must be thought.
WALT DISNEY	If you can dream it, you can do it.
VIRGIL	They can because they think they can.
T. S. ELIOT	Sometimes things become possible if we want them bad enough.

SUCCESS IS . . .

CHARLIE BROWN:
What do you want to
be when you grow up?

LINUS:
Outrageously happy!

UNKNOWN

A DIAMOND IS
MERELY A LUMP
OF COAL THAT
DID WELL UNDER
PRESSURE.

SUCCESS IS . . .

J. Paul Getty, oil executive and art collector, received a request from a magazine for a short article explaining his success. The billionaire obligingly wrote:

"SOME PEOPLE FIND OIL. OTHERS DON'T."

VINCE
LOMBARDI

Winning is a habit.
Unfortunately, so is losing.

WILL
DURANT

We are what we repeatedly do.
Excellence, then, is not an act,
but a habit.

ROBERT
COLLIER

Success is the sum of small efforts,
Repeated day in and day out.

SUCCESS IS . . .

WILLIAM
SHAKESPEARE

Our doubts are traitors
And make us lose the
good we oft might win
By fearing to attempt.

EDDIE
CANTOR

It takes twenty years to make
an overnight success.

HENRY DAVID THOREAU

IN THE LONG RUN, MEN HIT ONLY WHAT THEY AIM AT.

SUCCESS IS . . .

BENJAMIN FRANKLIN

EARLY TO BED AND
EARLY TO RISE, MAKES
A MAN HEALTHY,
WEALTHY, AND WISE.

JOHN MAYNARD
KEYNES

Ideas shape the course of history.

DAVID STARR
JORDAN

The world stands aside to let anyone
pass who knows where he is going.

SUCCESS IS . . .

THE ONLY LIMIT
TO OUR REALIZATION
OF TOMORROW
WILL BE OUR DOUBTS
OF TODAY.

YOU HAVE LOST
YOUR GOAL.
ALAS, HOW WILL
YOU DIGEST AND
JEST OVER THIS
LOSS? WITH THIS
YOU HAVE ALSO
LOST YOUR WAY.

SUCCESS IS . . .

WASHINGTON
IRVING

Little minds are subdued by misfortune;
but great minds rise above it.

VARIOUS

The harder I work, the luckier I get.

ESTÉE
LAUDER

I never dreamed about success,
I worked for it.

HARVEY MACKAY

PEOPLE BEGIN TO BECOME SUCCESSFUL THE MINUTE THEY DECIDE TO BE.

SUCCESS IS . . .

It's kind of fun to do the impossible.

SUCCESS IS...

. . . that old ABC—ability, breaks, and courage.

CHARLES LUCKMAN

. . . how high you bounce when you hit bottom.

GEORGE S. PATTON

. . . knowing your purpose in life, growing to reach your maximum potential, and sowing seeds that benefit others.

JOHN C. MAXWELL

. . . just a war of attrition. Sure, there's an element of talent you should probably possess. But if you just stick around long enough, eventually something is going to happen.

DAX SHEPARD

LARRY
WINGET

No one ever wrote down a plan to be fat, broke, stupid, lazy, unhappy, and mediocre. Those are the things that happen to you when you don't have a plan.

WAYNE
DYER

Be miserable. Or motivate yourself. Whatever has to be done, it's always your choice.

BONNIE
MCFARLANE

You know, women are burdened with all this other crap all the time, like looking good. You need to be really superhuman to be successful as a woman.

SUCCESS IS . . .

CRISS
JAMI

The biggest challenge after success
is shutting up about it.

HUBERT H.
HUMPHREY

Behind every successful man stands
a surprised mother-in-law.

PETER
DRUCKER

Wherever you see a successful business,
someone once made a courageous
decision.

DAVID STEINBERG

Success is . . .

When you're a baby success is not wetting your bed.

When you're a teenager success is going all the way.

When you're a young man success is making money.

When you are middle aged success is being happy.

When you're an old man success is going all the way.

And when you're really old it's not wetting your bed.

SUCCESS IS . . .

JACK CANFIELD

SUCCESS ISN'T MAGIC OR HOCUS-POCUS— IT'S SIMPLY LEARNING HOW TO FOCUS.

Walter Hagan, the first great golfing professional in the United States was asked the secret of his success.

"YOU'RE ONLY HERE FOR A SHORT VISIT, SO DON'T HURRY, DON'T WORRY, AND BE SURE TO SMELL THE FLOWERS ALONG THE WAY."

SUCCESS IS . . .

Financial consideration played only a small part in the satisfaction naturalist **John Muir** derived from life. On one occasion, he declared that he was richer than magnate E. H. Harriman:

"I HAVE ALL THE MONEY I WANT AND HE HASN'T."

SAMUEL JOHNSON	Great works are performed, not by strength, but perseverance.
JONATHAN SWIFT	Vision is the art of seeing things invisible.
JOHN IRVING	Half my life is an act of revision.
MARIAN WRIGHT EDELMAN	You're not obligated to win. You're obligated to keep trying to do the best you can do every day.

CARL JUNG

THE SHOE THAT FITS
ONE PERSON PINCHES
ANOTHER; THERE IS
NO UNIVERSAL RECIPE
FOR LIVING.

DOLLY PARTON

The way I see it, if you want the rainbow, you gotta put up with the rain.

LILY TOMLIN

The road to success is always under construction.

SENECA THE YOUNGER

If one does not know to which port one is sailing, no wind is favorable.

GEORGE R. KIRKPATRICK

Nature gave us two ends—one to sit on and one to think with.

SUCCESS IS . . .

WILL
SMITH

Being realistic is the most commonly traveled road to mediocrity.

ABRAHAM
LINCOLN

I do the very best I know how—the very best I can; and I mean to keep on doing so until the end.

THOMAS
JEFFERSON

I like the dreams of the future better than the history of the past.

The greatest things ever done on earth,
have been done by little and little.

THOMAS GUTHRIE

It's in our attitude,
our style, the way we talk, even.
Being yourself is the best path
to your own success.

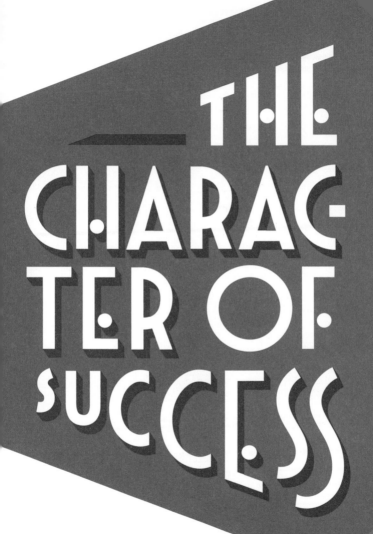

THE CHARAC-TER OF SUCCESS

CONSULT NOT
YOUR FEARS,
BUT YOUR HOPES
AND YOUR
DREAMS. THINK
NOT ABOUT YOUR
FRUSTRATIONS,
BUT ABOUT
YOUR UNFILLED
POTENTIAL.

THE CHARACTER OF SUCCESS

UTA HAGEN

WE MUST OVERCOME
THE NOTION THAT WE
MUST BE *REGULAR*. . . .
IT ROBS YOU OF
THE CHANCE TO BE
EXTRAORDINARY.

ANGELINA JOLIE

Figure out who you are separate from your family and the man or woman you're in a relationship with. Find who you are in this world and what you need to feel good alone. I think that's the most important thing in life. Find a sense of self because with that, you can do anything else.

OLIVER WENDELL HOLMES SR.

Have the courage to act instead of react.

HENRY STANLEY HASKINS

What lies behind us and what lies before us are tiny matters compared to what lies within us.

TERENCE	Fortune favors the brave.
SUGAR RAY ROBINSON	To be a champ you have to believe in yourself when nobody else will.
CLAIR OLIVER	Society may predict, but only I can determine my destiny.

THERE ARE ALL
THESE MOMENTS
YOU DON'T
THINK YOU
WILL SURVIVE.
AND THEN YOU
SURVIVE.

THE CHARACTER OF SUCCESS

OCTAVIA
E. BUTLER

In order to rise from its own ashes,
a phoenix first must burn.

MADELEINE
L'ENGLE

If we are not willing to fail, we will
never accomplish anything.

ERICH
FROMM

Creativity requires the courage
to let go of certainties.

JOHN
MASON

You were born an original.
Don't die a copy.

JUDY
GARLAND

Always be a first-rate version of yourself,
instead of a second-rate version of
somebody else.

RICK
OWENS

The coolest thing is when you don't care
about being cool anymore.

THE CHARACTER OF SUCCESS

BERNARD BARUCH

THOSE WHO MATTER
DON'T MIND,
AND THOSE WHO MIND
DON'T MATTER.

ECKHART TOLLE

You can only lose something that you have, but you cannot lose something that you are.

ADMIRAL WILLIAM HALSEY JR.

There are no great men, there are only great challenges, which ordinary men like you and me are forced by circumstances to meet.

MILES DAVIS

Man, sometimes it takes you a long time to sound like yourself.

NORTON JUSTER
The Phantom Tollbooth

. . . so many things are possible just as long as you don't know they're impossible.

THE CHARACTER OF SUCCESS

You have brains in your head.
You have feet in your shoes.
You can steer yourself any
direction you choose.
You're on your own, and you
know what you know.
And you are the guy who'll
decide where to go.

Change will not come if we wait for some other person or if we wait for some other time.

We are the ones we've been waiting for.

We are the change that we seek.

VICTOR
HUGO

Do not let it be your aim to be
something, but to be someone.

APPLE INC.

The people who are crazy enough
to think they can change the world,
are the ones who do.

BILLY
WILDER

Trust your own instinct. Your mistakes might as well be your own, instead of somebody else's.

RALPH WALDO
EMERSON

Every man is an impossibility until he is born.

CHRISTOPHER
MCDOUGALL

You're tougher than you think you are, and you can do more than you think you can.

MALCOLM
FORBES

Too many people overvalue what they are not and undervalue what they are.

WILFRID
NOYCE

We felt, too, that we had in no way "conquered" the mountain. We had conquered nothing except unruly bits of ourselves.

J. PAUL
GETTY

No one can possibly achieve any real and lasting success or "get rich" in business by being a conformist.

GEORGE
CARLIN

Those who dance are considered insane
by those who can't hear the music.

JOAN
RIVERS

I succeeded by saying what everyone
else is thinking.

ANNA
QUINDLEN

The thing that is really hard, and really
amazing, is giving up on being perfect
and beginning the work of becoming
yourself.

THE CHARACTER OF SUCCESS

CARL BUEHNER

THEY MAY FORGET
WHAT YOU SAID—
BUT THEY WILL NEVER
FORGET HOW YOU
MADE THEM FEEL.

IF PEOPLE DID NOT SOMETIMES DO SILLY THINGS, NOTHING INTELLIGENT WOULD EVER GET DONE.

COCO
CHANEL

In order to be irreplaceable one
must always be different.

ANONYMOUS

Be yourself.
Everyone else is already taken.

LUCILLE
BALL

Love yourself first and everything
falls into line.

MARTIN LUTHER KING JR.

THE ULTIMATE MEASURE
OF A MAN IS NOT
WHERE HE STANDS IN
MOMENTS OF COMFORT
AND CONVENIENCE,
BUT WHERE HE
STANDS AT TIMES OF
CHALLENGES AND
CONTROVERSY.

THE CHARACTER OF SUCCESS

ELEANOR ROOSEVELT

Do what you feel in your heart
to be right—for you'll be criticized
anyway. You'll be damned if you do,
and damned if you don't.

VINCENT VAN GOGH	Normality is a paved road. It's comfortable to walk, but no flowers grow.
ADELAIDE ANNE PROCTER	We always may be what we might have been.
JOHNNY CASH	If you aren't gonna say exactly how and what you feel, you might as well not say anything at all.

HENRY DAVID
THOREAU

Dreams are the touchstones
of our characters.

JOHN F.
KENNEDY

We need men who can dream
of things that never were.

J. K. ROWLING
Harry Potter and the Chamber of Secrets

It is our choices . . . that show what we truly are, far more than our abilities.

JOHN WOODEN

Be more concerned with your character than your reputation. Character is what you really are. Reputation is what people say you are.

WILLIAM J. H. BOETCKER

The individual activity of one man with backbone will do more than a thousand men with a mere wishbone.

THE CHARACTER OF SUCCESS

LET ME TELL YOU
THE SECRET THAT HAS
LED ME TO MY GOAL:
MY STRENGTH LIES
SOLELY IN MY TENACITY.

EVERY MINUTE OF
EVERY HOUR OF EVERY
DAY YOU ARE MAKING
THE WORLD, JUST
AS YOU ARE MAKING
YOURSELF, AND YOU
MIGHT AS WELL DO IT
WITH GENEROSITY AND
KINDNESS AND STYLE.

THE CHARACTER OF SUCCESS

| MARK TWAIN | Keep away from people who try to belittle your ambitions. Small people always do. |

| A. W. TOZER | Refuse to be average. |

| PROVERB | Great oaks from little acorns grow. |

JERRY LEWIS	I've had great success being a total idiot.
HENRY DAVID THOREAU	What a man thinks of himself, that it is which determines, or rather indicates, his fate.
HENRY DAVID THOREAU	If one advances confidently in the direction of his own dreams and endeavors to live the life that he has imagined, he will meet with a success unexpected in common hours.
PROVERB	If you want to be respected, you must respect yourself.

THE CHARACTER OF SUCCESS

BOBBY
MCFERRIN

Don't worry, be happy.

CECIL
BEATON

Be daring, be different,
be impractical, be anything that
will assert integrity of purpose
and imaginative vision against
the play-it-safers, the creatures
of the commonplace, the slaves
of the ordinary.

BENJAMIN SPOCK

TRUST YOURSELF. YOU KNOW MORE THAN YOU THINK YOU DO.

MAX
DE PREE

We cannot become what we need
to be by remaining what we are.

JAMES
ALLEN

Circumstance does not make the man,
it reveals him to himself.

DOLLY
PARTON

If your actions create a legacy that
inspires others to dream more, learn
more, do more and become more,
then, you are an excellent leader.

CHER	All of us invent ourselves. Some of us just have more imagination than others.
US ARMY	Be all you can be.
WILLIAM MAKEPEACE THACKERAY	Whatever you are, try to be a good one.

ELEANOR ROOSEVELT

REMEMBER ALWAYS
THAT YOU NOT
ONLY HAVE THE
RIGHT TO BE AN
INDIVIDUAL, YOU
HAVE AN OBLIGATION
TO BE ONE.

Character cannot be developed in ease and quiet. Only through experience of trial and suffering can the soul be strengthened, vision cleared, ambition inspired, and success achieved.

HELEN KELLER

The life well lived is the one that
feels like a success at the end of the day.
And that takes many forms whether in
deeds or words or even thoughts.

WILLIAM
JAMES
The great use of life is to spend
it for something that outlasts it.

HELICE
BRIDGES
I am not just here to make a living;
I am here to make a life.

GOLDA
MEIR
Trust yourself. Create the kind of self
that you will be happy with all your life.

TIME IS THE COIN OF YOUR LIFE. IT IS THE ONLY COIN YOU HAVE, AND ONLY YOU CAN DETERMINE HOW IT WILL BE SPENT.

HENRY DAVID
THOREAU

The price of anything is the amount
of life you exchange for it.

LEO
BUSCAGLIA

Don't brood. Get on with living and
loving. You don't have forever.

SAINT EDMUND
OF ABINGDON

Study as if you were to live for ever;
live as if you were to die tomorrow.

JONATHAN
SWIFT

May you live all the days of your life.

LIFE IS...

. . . a succession of lessons which must be lived to be understood.

RALPH WALDO EMERSON

. . . too short to be little.

BENJAMIN DISRAELI

. . . half spent, before we know what it is.

GEORGE HERBERT

. . . really simple, but men insist on making it complicated.

CONFUCIUS

. . . either a daring adventure or nothing at all.

HELEN KELLER

. . . just what happens to you, while you're busy making other plans.

JOHN LENNON

ANDY ROONEY

For most of life, nothing wonderful happens. If you don't enjoy getting up and working and finishing your work and sitting down to a meal with family or friends, then the chances are you're not going to be very happy. If someone bases his/her happiness on major events like a great job, huge amounts of money, a flawlessly happy marriage or a trip to Paris, that person isn't going to be happy much of the time. If, on the other hand, happiness depends on a good breakfast, flowers in the yard, a drink or a nap, then we are more likely to live with quite a bit of happiness.

SUCCESS IN LIFE

CHRISTOPHER
MORLEY

There is only one success . . .
to be able to spend your life in
your own way.

HENRY DAVID
THOREAU

If one advances confidently in the
direction of his dreams, and endeavors
to live the life which he has imagined,
he will meet with a success unexpected
in common hours.

MARCUS
AURELIUS

Very little indeed is necessary
for living a happy life.

JOSH
BILLINGS

Life consists not in holding good cards
but in playing those you hold well.

VIVIAN
GREENE

Life isn't about waiting for the storms
to pass. It's about learning how to dance
in the rain.

UNKNOWN   The two hardest things to handle
                 in life are failure and success.

QUENTIN   If at first you don't succeed, failure may
CRISP   be your style.

MALCOLM
FORBES

When you cease to dream
you cease to live.

TIM
KIZZIAR

Our greatest fear . . . should
not be of failure but of
succeeding at things in life
that don't really matter.

GAIL
SHEEHY

If we don't change,
we don't grow.
If we don't grow,
we aren't really living.

SIGMUND FREUD

It is impossible to escape the impression that people commonly use false standards of measurement— that they seek power, success and wealth for themselves and admire them in others, and that they underestimate what is of true value in life.

JOHN
GREEN

What is the point of being alive if
you don't at least try to do something
remarkable?

NELSON
MANDELA

There is no passion to be found playing
small—in settling for a life that is less
than the one you are capable of living.

SUCCESS IN LIFE

LOVE THE LIFE
YOU LIVE.
LIVE THE LIFE
YOU LOVE.

SUCCESS IS FINDING SATISFACTION IN GIVING A LITTLE MORE THAN YOU TAKE.

VICTOR
HUGO

The greatest happiness of life is the
conviction that we are loved; loved
for ourselves, or rather, loved in spite
of ourselves.

THOMAS
MERTON

We do not find the meaning of life by
ourselves alone—we find it with another.

Your time is limited, so don't waste it living someone else's life. Don't be trapped by dogma—which is living with the results of other people's thinking. Don't let the noise of others' opinion drown out your own inner voice. And most important, have the courage to follow your heart and intuition. They somehow already know what you truly want to become.

THE ART OF LIVING IS MORE LIKE WRESTLING THAN DANCING.

RALPH WALDO EMERSON

ALL LIFE IS AN EXPERIMENT. THE MORE EXPERIMENTS YOU MAKE THE BETTER.

SUCCESS IN LIFE

RICHARD B. GUNDERMAN

WE MAKE A LIVING BY WHAT WE GET, BUT WE MAKE A LIFE BY WHAT WE GIVE.

He has achieved success who has lived well,
laughed often, and loved much;

Who has enjoyed the trust of pure women, the respect
of intelligent men and the love of little children;

Who has filled his niche and accomplished
his task;

Who has never lacked appreciation of Earth's beauty
or failed to express it;

Who has left the world better than he found it,

Whether an improved poppy, a perfect poem,
or a rescued soul;

Who has always looked for the best in others and given
them the best he had;

Whose life was an inspiration;

Whose memory a benediction.

BESSIE ANDERSON STANLEY

It is through failure that
we're able to see more clearly and
enjoy more abundantly our successes.
Failure is how we learn and what
reminds us of our humanity.

THE IMPOR- TANCE OF FAILURE

WILLIAM
SLOANE

Publication is not necessarily a sign of success.

SCOTT
ADAMS

Creativity is allowing yourself to make mistakes. Art is knowing which ones to keep.

BRENDA
UELAND

Inspiration does not come like a bolt, nor is it kinetic energy striving, but it comes into us slowly and quietly and all the time.

THE IMPORTANCE OF FAILURE

CASSANDRA CLARE

Hope is not illusion.

ZORA NEALE HURSTON

There are years that ask questions and years that answer.

IF I HAD TO LIVE
MY LIFE AGAIN
I'D MAKE THE
SAME MISTAKES—
ONLY SOONER.

THE IMPORTANCE OF FAILURE

DENIS WAITLEY

Forget about the consequences of failure. Failure is only a temporary change in direction to set you straight for your next success.

The real test is not whether you avoid this failure, because you won't. It's whether you let it harden or shame you into inaction, or whether you learn from it; whether you choose to persevere.

MICHAEL JORDAN

I've missed more than 9,000 shots in my career. I've lost almost 300 games. Twenty-six times, I've been trusted to take the game-winning shot and missed. I've failed over and over and over again in my life. And that is why I succeed.

BABE RUTH

Every strike brings me closer to the next home run.

THOMAS J. WATSON	If you want to succeed, double your failure rate.
MARY PICKFORD	This thing that we call failure is not the falling down, but the staying down.
RICHARD BRANSON	Do not be embarrassed by your failures, learn from them and start again.
THOMAS EDISON	I have not failed. I've just found 10,000 ways that won't work.

THE IMPORTANCE OF FAILURE

JAPANESE PROVERB	Fall seven times and stand up eight.
JOSEPH CHILTON PEARCE	To live a creative life, we must lose our fear of being wrong.

THEODORE ROOSEVELT	It is hard to fail, but it is worse never to have tried to succeed.
DEBBI FIELDS	The important thing is not being afraid to take a chance. Remember, the greatest failure is to not try.
FRIEDRICH NIETZSCHE	A thinker sees his own actions as experiments and questions as attempts to find out something. Success and failure are for him answers above all.

THE IMPORTANCE OF FAILURE

ONLY THOSE WHO
DARE TO FAIL
GREATLY, CAN EVER
ACHIEVE GREATLY.

FAILURE IS...

. . . only the opportunity more intelligently to begin again.

HENRY FORD

. . . the stepping stone for success.

PROVERB

. . . the condiment that gives success its flavor.

TRUMAN CAPOTE

DOROTHEA BRANDE	Act as if it were impossible to fail.
DREW HOUSTON	Failure doesn't matter: you only have to be right once.
BENJAMIN FRANKLIN	There are no gains without pains.

JOSH BILLINGS

Success does not consist in never making mistakes but in never making the same one a second time.

PROVERB

Success in the end erases all the mistakes along the way.

FREDERICK DOUGLASS	If there is no struggle, there is no progress.
PROVERB	Smooth seas do not make skillful sailors.
ZIG ZIGLAR	Attitude is the little thing that makes the big difference.

THE IMPORTANCE OF FAILURE

JAMES CAMERON

IF YOU SET YOUR
GOALS RIDICULOUSLY
HIGH AND IT'S A
FAILURE, YOU WILL
FAIL ABOVE EVERYONE
ELSE'S SUCCESS.

PROVERB   Stumbling is not the same as falling.

UNKNOWN   Life's real failure is when you do not
                 realize how close you were to success
                 when you gave up.

THE IMPORTANCE OF FAILURE

EPICTETUS   It is difficulties that show what men are.

ELBERT   The greatest mistake you can make in
HUBBARD   your life is to be continually fearing that
                   you will make one.

L. M. MONTGOMERY

. . . TOMORROW
IS A NEW DAY
WITH NO MISTAKES
IN IT YET.

THE IMPORTANCE OF FAILURE

NELSON MANDELA

AFTER CLIMBING
A GREAT HILL,
ONE ONLY FINDS
THAT THERE ARE
MANY MORE HILLS
TO CLIMB.

STEVEN WRIGHT	If at first you don't succeed then skydiving definitely isn't for you.
STEVEN WRIGHT	If at first you don't succeed, destroy all evidence that you tried.
W. C. FIELDS	If at first you don't succeed, try, try again. Then quit. No use being a damn fool about it.

THE IMPORTANCE OF FAILURE

UNKNOWN

Success comes in cans;
failure in can'ts.

BEVERLY
SILLS

You may be disappointed
if you fail, but you are
doomed if you don't try.

THOMAS
EDISON

Many of life's failures are people
who did not realize how close
they were to success when
they gave up.

OLIVER
GOLDSMITH

Our greatest glory is not in never falling,
but in rising every time we fall.

AMY
POEHLER

You can't do it alone. . . . Other people
and other people's ideas are often better
than your own.

ANONYMOUS

Things work out best for those who
make the best of how things work out.

THE IMPORTANCE OF FAILURE

CHARLES DICKENS

I HAVE BEEN BENT AND BROKEN, BUT—I HOPE—INTO A BETTER SHAPE.

Try again.
Fail again.
Fail better.

SAMUEL BECKETT

Only in doing can we achieve,
and success in any form is an achievement.
So dare to achieve more, to try harder, to keep
going—that's what success is built on.

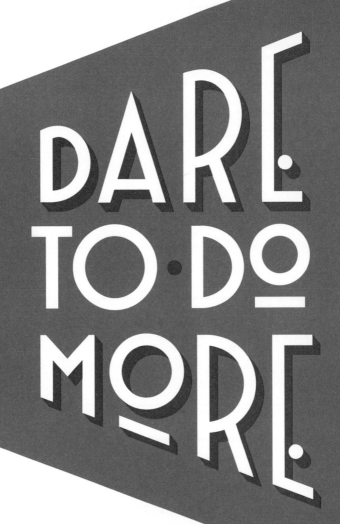

THE FIGHT IS WON OR LOST FAR AWAY FROM WITNESSES— BEHIND THE LINES, IN THE GYM, AND OUT THERE ON THE ROAD, LONG BEFORE I DANCE UNDER THOSE LIGHTS.

DARE TO DO MORE

When you get into a tight place, and everything goes against you till it seems as if you couldn't hang on a minute longer, *never give up then*, for that's just the place and time that the tide will turn.

THOMAS EDISON	There's a way to do it better.
UNKNOWN	Let sleeping dogs lie.
MAE JEMISON	Never limit yourself because of others' limited imagination; never limit others because of your own limited imagination.

DARE TO DO MORE

BENJAMIN
FRANKLIN

Either write things worth reading,
or do things worth the writing.

FRANCIS
BACON

A wise man will make more
opportunities than he finds.

MICHAEL
KORDA

To succeed it is necessary to accept the world as it is and rise above it.

LEON C.
MEGGINSON

It is not the most intellectual of the species that survives; it is not the strongest that survives; but the species that survives is the one that is able best to adapt and adjust to the changing environment in which it finds itself.

DARE TO DO MORE

IT IS NOT THE MAN
WHO HAS TOO LITTLE,
BUT THE MAN WHO
DESIRES MORE,
THAT IS POOR.

ANDRÉ GIDE

THERE ARE MANY
THINGS THAT
SEEM IMPOSSIBLE
ONLY SO LONG
AS ONE DOES NOT
ATTEMPT THEM.

DARE TO DO MORE

PETER
DRUCKER

Follow effective actions with quiet reflection. From the quiet reflection will come even more effective action.

DOE
ZANTAMATA

Taking time to do nothing often brings everything into perspective.

RALPH WALDO EMERSON	Always do what you are afraid to do.
MATSUO BASHŌ	Seek not to follow in the footsteps of men of old; seek what they sought.
UNKNOWN	The man who says it cannot be done should not interrupt the man doing it.

DARE TO DO MORE

ROY L.
SMITH

The successful man is the one who finds out what is the matter with his business before his competitors do.

CHUCK
CLOSE

Inspiration is for amateurs—the rest of us just show up and get to work.

A WOODSMAN WAS ONCE ASKED,

"What would you do if you had just five minutes to chop down a tree?"

HE ANSWERED,

"I would spend the first two and a half minutes sharpening my axe."

DARE TO DO MORE

ANATOLE FRANCE

TO ACCOMPLISH
GREAT THINGS,
WE MUST NOT ONLY
ACT, BUT ALSO DREAM,
NOT ONLY PLAN,
BUT ALSO BELIEVE.

VINCENT
VAN GOGH

Love many things, for therein lies
the true strength, and whosoever
loves much performs much, and
can accomplish much, and what
is done in love is well done.

H. JACKSON
BROWN JR.

Remember that everyone you
meet is afraid of something,
loves something, and has lost
something.

DARE TO DO MORE

STEPHEN HAWKING

Try to make sense of what you see and wonder about what makes the universe exist. Be curious, and however difficult life may seem, there is always something you can do, and succeed at. It matters that you don't just give up.

OBSERVE THE
POSTAGE STAMP—
ITS USEFULNESS
DEPENDS UPON
ITS ABILITY TO
STICK TO ONE
THING TILL
IT GETS THERE.

UNKNOWN

THINGS MAY COME
TO THOSE WHO
WAIT, BUT ONLY THE
THINGS LEFT BY
THOSE WHO HUSTLE.

JOHN STEINBECK	Ideas are like rabbits. You get a couple, and learn how to handle them, and pretty soon you have a dozen.
FRANCIS BACON	Knowledge itself is power.
UNKNOWN	Every survival kit should include a sense of humor.

DARE TO DO MORE

RENÉ
DESCARTES

It is not enough to have a good mind;
the important thing is to use it well.

BERTRAND
RUSSELL

The good life is one inspired by love
and guided by knowledge.

Take up one idea. Make that one idea your life—think of it, dream of it, live on that idea. Let the brain, muscles, nerves, every part of your body, be full of that idea, and just leave every other idea alone.

CARL
BARD

Though no one can go back and make
a brand-new start, anyone can start from
now and make a brand-new ending.

T. S.
ELIOT

Only those who will risk going too
far can possibly find out how far one
can go.

DAVID
BLY

Striving for success without hard work is like trying to harvest where you haven't planted.

DONALD M.
KENDALL

The only place where success comes before work is in the dictionary.

ALEXANDER
GRAHAM BELL

Before anything else, preparation is the key to success.

DARE TO DO MORE

HITCH YOUR WAGON TO A STAR.

YOU...

. . . will fail at some point in your life. . . . Sometimes it's the best way to figure out where you're going.

DENZEL WASHINGTON

. . . have to trust in something—your gut, destiny, life, karma, whatever. This approach has never let me down, and it has made all the difference in my life.

STEVE JOBS

. . . don't have to see the whole staircase, just take the first step.

MARTIN LUTHER KING JR.

. . . miss 100% of the shots you don't take.

WAYNE GRETZKY

. . . see things; and you say "Why?" But I dream things that never were; and I say "Why not?"

GEORGE BERNARD SHAW

I BELIEVE THAT
THE ONLY COURAGE
ANYBODY EVER NEEDS
IS THE COURAGE
TO FOLLOW YOUR
OWN DREAMS.

DARE TO DO MORE

JOHN F. KENNEDY

EFFORT AND COURAGE ARE NOT ENOUGH WITHOUT PURPOSE AND DIRECTION.

GEORGE HORACE LORIMER

You've got to get up every morning with determination if you're going to go to bed with satisfaction.

THOMAS EDISON

When I have fully decided that a result is worth getting, I go about it, and make trial after trial, until it comes.

H. JACKSON BROWN JR.

Twenty years from now you will be more disappointed by the things that you didn't do than by the ones you did do. So throw off the bowlines. Sail away from the safe harbor. Catch the trade winds in your sails. Explore. Dream. Discover.

DARE TO DO MORE

UNKNOWN

The best way to succeed in this world is to act on the advice you give to others.

G. K. CHESTERTON

I owe my success to having listened respectfully and rather bashfully to the very best advice . . . and then going away and doing the exact opposite.

ALBERT EINSTEIN

Imagination is more important than knowledge.

BENJAMIN FRANKLIN

It is not only right to strike while the iron is hot, but that it may be very practicable to heat it by continually striking.

DARE TO DO MORE

RANDY
PAUSCH

Time is all you have. And you may find one day that you have less than you think.

PATTI
DIGH

The death rate for people who play it safe and for people who live boldly is the same: 100%.

PEOPLE MAY DOUBT WHAT YOU SAY, BUT THEY WILL BELIEVE WHAT YOU DO.

RALPH WALDO EMERSON	Every artist was first an amateur.
LIVY	Better late than never.
TONY HSIEH	Stop chasing the money and start chasing the passion.

GRACE HANSEN

Don't be afraid your life will end;
Be afraid that it will never begin.

MORRIS WEST

If you spend your whole life waiting
for the storm, you'll never enjoy the
sunshine.

VERONICA ROTH

Becoming fearless isn't the point.
That's impossible. It's learning how
to control your fear, and how to be
free from it.

DARE TO DO MORE

LAO-TZU

A journey of a thousand miles must begin with a single step.

NAPOLEON
HILL

Do not wait. The time will never be "just right."

CONAN O'BRIEN

IT IS OUR FAILURE
TO BECOME OUR
PERCEIVED IDEAL
THAT ULTIMATELY
DEFINES US AND
MAKES US UNIQUE. . . .
YOUR PERCEIVED
FAILURE CAN BECOME
A CATALYST FOR
PROFOUND
REINVENTION.

DARE TO DO MORE

HERMAN
MELVILLE

It is better to fail in originality, than to succeed in imitation.

OPRAH
WINFREY

Learn from every mistake . . . and then, figure out what is the next right move.

Nothing in the world can
take the place of persistence.

Talent will not; nothing is more
common than unsuccessful
men with talent.

Genius will not; unrewarded genius
is almost a proverb.

Education will not; the world
is full of educated derelicts.

Persistence and determination
alone are omnipotent.

The slogan "press on" has solved
and always will solve the problems
of the human race.

DARE TO DO MORE

| CARRIE FISHER | Instant gratification takes too long. |
| GUSTAVE FLAUBERT | Talent is long patience, and originality an effort of will and of intense observation. |

JACK
LONDON

Don't loaf and invite inspiration;
light out after it with a club, and if you
don't get it you will nonetheless get
something that looks remarkably like it.

OG
MANDINO

Always will I take another step.
If that is of no avail, I will take another,
and yet another.

LUDWIG VAN
BEETHOVEN

I want to seize fate by the throat.

DARE TO DO MORE

ANAÏS NIN

And the day came when the risk to remain tight in a bud was more painful than the risk it took to blossom.

ANDREW JACKSON

Take time to deliberate; but when the time for action arrives, stop thinking and go in.

WALTER HELLER

Rise above principle and do what's right.

UNKNOWN · Success isn't just about what you accomplish in your life; it's about what you inspire others to do.

OLIVER WENDELL HOLMES SR. · The great thing in this world is not so much where we stand, as in what direction we are moving.

UNKNOWN · The difference between who you are and who you want to be is what you do.

ANDRÉ GIDE · One doesn't discover new lands without consenting to lose sight of the shore for a very long time.

DARE TO DO MORE

WINSTON
CHURCHILL

Success always demands
a greater effort.

HERMANN
HESSE

Only the ideas we actually live
are of any value.

DAN MILLMAN
Peaceful Warrior

The journey is what brings us happiness,
not the destination.

Here is your life. You might never have been, but you are because the party wouldn't have been complete without you. Here is the world. Beautiful and terrible things will happen.

FREDERICK BUECHNER

THE SECRET OF SUCCESS...

. . . in life is for a man to be ready for his opportunity when it comes.

BENJAMIN DISRAELI

. . . is to do the common thing uncommonly well.

JOHN D. ROCKEFELLER JR.

. . . is constancy to purpose.

BENJAMIN DISRAELI

. . . is this: **There is no secret of success.**

ELBERT HUBBARD

This book is dedicated to Dash Darcy.
Wishing you a lifetime of successes,
however you choose to define them.

Always in your corner, H.N.

Design by Hana Anouk Nakamura
Custom typography by Nick Misani

ISBN: 978-1-4197-3399-4

Foreword © 2019 Lindsey Pollak

© 2019 Abrams

Printed and bound in China

10 9 8 7 6 5 4 3 2 1

Abrams Noterie products are available at special discounts when
purchased in quantity for premiums and promotions as well as fundraising
or educational use. Special editions can also be created to specification.
For details, contact specialsales@abramsbooks.com or the address below.

Abrams Noterie® is a registered trademark of Harry N. Abrams, Inc.

ABRAMS The Art of Books
195 Broadway, New York, NY 10007
abramsbooks.com

FSC
www.fsc.org
MIX
Paper from
responsible sources
FSC™ C101537